Don't pet the plants!

Written by Rachel Delahaye

Illustrated by Lee Teng

Collins

Last week my little sister, Grace, asked for a pet.
She tried everything.

"I want something to play with!" Grace wailed. "Please!"

Mum said, "Pets are not playthings. They're a commitment. They need lots of attention and our family is just too busy."

"I'm sad, Ollie," Grace sobbed, miserably.

"Cuddly toys can be pets," I suggested, helpfully.

"But I want something living!" she wept.

"Plants are alive." I pointed to my treasured cactus.

"Oh!" she said, and instantly brightened up.

The next morning Dad whispered, "Marvellous idea, Ollie," and took Grace to a garden shop.

Later, I knocked on her bedroom door ...

Wow! Plants were everywhere! And some were exceedingly big – even taller than me!

Grace introduced each one:

Magnificent, the climbing jungle vine,

Bungle the cheese plant with gaps in his leaves,

Bouncy the spider plant with stripy fronds,

Misty the bushy fern, and Loopy – tree-like with a huge trunk.

And *so* many others, I forgot their names.

Grace smiled and rolled her eyes.
"They are such characters!"

The next day, the plants had grown massively.

I stroked a gigantic one and Grace snapped, "Don't pet the plants!"

"These are not *playthings*, you know," she said. "They're a *commitment*."

Grace's pets grew so speedily – taller, bigger, wider, longer …
Her room was like a huge plant kingdom!

I think she sometimes had difficulty finding her way out,
because some days we didn't see her for hours.

She spent all her time ...

... watering

... measuring

... inspecting for fleas (I think she meant aphids)

... carefully following the instructions on the labels.

She even read plant books all by herself, to make sure she didn't do anything wrong.

Then one day, her fern started wilting. She paced up and down.

"Aha!" she said. "Tropical plants need heat! The fern is probably cold!"

She turned up the heating.

We had to eat dinner in our coolest clothes because the house was sweltering.

Yesterday, we noticed a strange scent upstairs.
It was a concoction of damp earth
and rotting leaves. It probably stank
worse than a wet dog.

16

Mum and Dad had a discussion.

Today, we've told Grace that we're taking her shopping to choose an extra-special plant.

But we're not.

Shhh, it's a surprise!

"We're very proud of your passion and dedication," Mum says.

"But we can't stand the smell," adds Dad.

19

We take home a pair of gerbils and call them Crumb and Sugar.

My job is feeding. Dad's is cleaning. Mum's doing hutch construction.

Grace?

I'm sure you've worked it out ... She's in charge of giving them attention.

Plenty of attention.

Can you introduce Grace's plants?

Magnificent
climbing vine

Misty
bushy fern

Bouncy
spider plant
with stripy fronds

22

Loopy
tree-like, with a large trunk

Bungle
cheese plant
with gaps in his leaves

 After reading

Letters and Sounds: Phases 5–6

Word count: 497

Focus phonemes: /n/ kn /m/ mb /r/ wr /s/ c, ce, sc /zh/ s /sh/ ti, ci, ssi, s

Common exception words: of, to, the, are, said, do, were, one, our, oh, their, today, says, door, because, busy, watering, many, anything, hours, eyes, whole

Curriculum links: Science: Plants

National Curriculum learning objectives: Reading/word reading: apply phonic knowledge and skills as the route to decode words, read common exception words, noting unusual correspondences between spelling and sound and where these occur in the word; read other words of more than one syllable that contain taught GPCs; Reading/comprehension: develop pleasure in reading, motivation to read, vocabulary and understanding by being encouraged to link what they read or hear to their own experiences

Developing fluency

- Your child may enjoy hearing you read the book.
- Take turns to read a page of the main text, encouraging the use of different voices for each character and expression of feelings through tone.

Phonic practice

- Challenge your child to identify the /s/ or /sh/ sounds in each of these words with more than one syllable.

  magnificent   construction   concoction   exceedingly   Sugar

- Can they identify the word with four syllables? (ex/ceed/ing/ly)

Extending vocabulary

- Challenge your child to think of other words they can make using the following, by adding an ending, such as -ing, -ed, -ion, -y, -ment. Can they spell them correctly?

  bounce (e.g. *bouncy, bounced*)   discuss (*discussing, discussion*)

  commit (*committed, commitment*)